BITS AND PIECES

SAMIR ARJUN SHARMA

Thank you, Universe, and much love to my family and friends.

Love you Ama!

I want to sincerely express my love to Shivansh, Yash, and Agastya!

Contents

Foreword

When asked how he describes himself being an author and a poet, he answered;-

From my bed to my grave I shall write,
I shall be my first critic and last reader.

He further added, 'the bits and pieces I create are beyond humiliation or appreciation and the glory of my written words shall be reflected only after I am gone to the dust from where I had come.

I seek pleasure in these words I write and I find my pride within it and no paradise can lure me to give up writing.

Preface

Books by this author;

The last dream, Tears & rain, The old scars, I killed in the name of love and the Unknown.

The illusionist is back and this time he has to offer poems which is a blend of his imagination and his early days of rootless spiritual wandering tales.

Acknowledgements

Thank you, Universe, and my sincere gratitude towards you!

I want to thank my family and friends for their blend of appreciation and criticism which initially helped me start this project (A series including 7 books of poems and quotes to be published accordingly).

Note: Criticism is a very crucial key and is as important as appreciation.

Prologue

The author has made this significantly clear that he has covered various niches in this very book and as well as the upcoming books will feature poems and short stories which will have diverse bits and pieces to keep the readers engrossed and entertained.

1. Unfortunately 'Us'

Mental illness can be of several kinds but those suffering should be treated with love and care let alone with respect and honor as the battle they are fighting may not be visible to naked eyes but it is indeed one of the hardest battles to fight.

This poem is a tribute to all those who had passed away, those currently struggling, and those who had overcome any sort of mental illness.

Unfortunately 'Us'
I have a brother living within me,
slowly, and eventually, he and I became we.
I tried to let him go, but he comes back again,
making me believe that he isn't going anywhere,
not until I turn insane.
Since I was a kid, he did live within me,
and he did all the insignificant things,
though the blame was on me.
I do believe he is stronger than me?
Yet don't you think it is weird because,
he is just an illusion created by no one but me.
I cry at times and smile again,
and he is happy to see me in pain.
I am not immortal neither is he,
the day I shall be gone,
so shall be he.
I am a poet and I express my sorrows in words,

he is a devil always ready to hurt me with a sword.

I may be gone soon as my time has come,

but while I wave the final goodbye,

I wonder, along with the crowd will he also come,

this time similarly with weed, whiskey, or rum?

You say my mind is not stable,

so why don't you do me a favor,

let me live a day without you,

I shall be in debt to you forever.

Tonight might be the last day of my life,

it is indeed better to die than to live on the edge of a knife.

Once I am gone so shall be you,

but I will return soon,

next time without you.

2. Walk in the Park

The bond between a mother and her son is undying and true, and when one loses his mother at an early age he is for sure broken from within. This poem is a dedication to all the beautiful mothers on earth and in heaven.

Walk in the Park

I remember the last walk with my mother in the park,

we started the walk around the dusk that went on until the sky turned dark.

She spoke to me those words which still rhyme in my ears,

as she has gone far away from me yet her words of wisdom nonetheless help me to fight my fears.

My son she whispered and told me life isn't always fair,

asked me never lose that one person who would truly love me;

As someone loving us with a sincere heart these days is rigorously rare.

She knew she didn't have many days to live yet she looked so gracious and in bliss,

I still remember that moment when her gracious body was lying on the pyre; I whispered, 'Mother you shall be forever missed'.

She wasn't extensively educated, nevertheless, her wisdom truly matched her beauty,

she often told me that becoming a kind and humble man should be one's life goal and duty.

I remember while growing up we weren't affluent but we were content,

she taught me life is not meant for quarrels but one should be keen on finding ways to mend.

Today as I walk the path of adulthood, I seek no treasure or holy grail,

all I wish is to build a ship that shall help me to go back to my childhood days,

where my mother would speak of those undying tales of courage and wisdom;

That is where I desire to go and forever sail.

3. O my heart; My poor heart

Somewhere in Kerela, the rootless wanderer was wandering amidst the beautiful nature; While expressing and getting inspired at the same time by the magnificent and mesmerizing beauty of the city he was in, the wanderer read something which caught his eyes and, it read,
"Don't come to my grave with flowers in your hand & tears in your eyes,
Instead,
Come now and save my soul".

O my heart; My poor heart
Why do we grieve over a lost love when we know relationships are futile?
Why do we cross the ocean for those while they choose not to cross a mile?
Oh, my heart you innocent one why does it bleed for her as she is already gone,
why would you still wish her to return; Haven't you already mourned?
Look around you fool and embrace the pain while you move on,
pick up a new hobby of some kind or rather end your life at once with that lineal gun.
Yesterday is history while tomorrow is a mystery to unfold,
why in heaven would you not live in present and be bold.
What wrong did you do as you weep every night,
all you did was loved her truly; Just to save her from yourself,
you had to struggle for ages, ain't that right?.

Worry none my poor heart as your pain shall be gone soon far,

little your beloved woman would realize that you had loved her so dearly though from afar.

The shipman has arrived and he is waiting for you at the river Styx and he is in rush for sure,

it is a hidden truth for ages as love is that very poison that has no cure.

There you go my mate oh my dear old friend as you did suffer a lot for real and for nothingness;

But in reality, it wasn't the suffering of the present but the memories of the past for you couldn't ask for forgiveness.

Goodbye, my brother in arms as we shall never be united again for you are mortal and I am not,

but you shall be dearly loved where you are heading;

As my heart, you were wrongly sent to earth and that is why you had to rot.

4. Religion: - Be kind to me

While the spiritual wanderer was on his quest to find the path of his holiness; He often met people of every caste, religion, and race but never found any difference in anyone of them as all sought love consciously or unconsciously.

Religion: - Be kind to me

The son of the sun loved the daughter of the moon;

Neither of them was aware of their fate and where they were heading soon.

Religious monuments were once known to be devoted to sharing the word of love and peace;

Now their self-acclaimed protectors aren't having mercy on either nephew or niece.

God is one but do we sincerely care;

Respecting one and respecting all is a philosophy that is followed by real gems that are found very rare.

The couple in love realized their so-called family wouldn't spare them for committing such a big sin which involved love, emotions, and sincere feelings;

As their loved ones were only concerned about their blind fate on orthodox beliefs which may only be satisfied with killings.

They decided to remain in love even after death and seek salvation;

They stabbed each other without realizing for a bit that wasn't a path to liberation.

Today while wandering around the streets, I landed up to their grave;
I overheard an old couple gossiping about those sun and moon offspring and the tale about how their souls may still crave.
Let's not kill each other in the name of religion as God is one and is kind,
Better to be a Gopal saving Nazia and Ahmed saving Radhika as that was the true preaching of the almighty if we all think from our heart and mind.

5. Dilemma

'Memento Mori', is often used by those who follow Stoicism. It states "Remember that you will die", which simply means one should know that he is not immortal.

Lord Gautam Buddha once said the problem with humans is we think we have enough time but the fact is no one knows or can be sure how much time we do have for real.

The below-written poem is a dedication to those who had worked hard to achieve their dreams and goals and to those who had to give up their dreams for the sake of earning their livelihood.

Dilemma

It was such a beautiful night and he was staring at the stars from his balcony; Wondered to himself how can life be so uncanny.

What had he gained by being kind he often asks his former self;

He is still stuck to his eight years old self who heartily believed in wonderland and elves.

Growing up was hard and he had to fight every day and struggle through every night;

He often thought to himself; Was seeking some love and care wasn't even his right?

Then came the day which turned the kid into a warrior and he turned brutal;

He took his chances every now and then which brought him success but sometimes they were likely fatal.

From sinking in his own ship to building a mesmerizing castle he had seen it all;
Some days he was seen as way too enthusiastic or vibrant and at days he was simply dull.
But he never gave up fighting with his own destiny as he was destined to win;
He was a man of honor but to gain victory he often had to commit sins.
From being broke and burned to becoming brave and successful he came a long way ahead;
It was his demons within which did stop him at times but again they were what truly lead.
He cried and fell and stood up again;
He was often seen to be insane;
But if we think wisely; Is there anyone in this world who is sincerely sane?
With nothing but his dreams and undying faith in self he created his empire;
He can still feel the wrath of pain and sorrow burning inside him as the everlasting fire.
Today he has everything that a man would seek or ask;
Little did his loved ones know how sad he was from within; But outside he was wearing a smile and laughter mask.
From being that poor eight-year kid to a wealthy and famous eighty-year man he did everything which had to be done;
He never received a flower while he breathes but he shall when he would be finally gone.
Staring at those stars he can feel a sense of victory for sure;
But he also has resentments for things he committed as he prayed to

God but also to the devil he has to lure.

Now he is living his last days on earth as he is diagnosed with this illness which has no cure;

But he has no regrets as he did everything to become the man who he once dreamt to become and after dying he shall be in peace for sure.

By the time I am done writing this poem I shall have this dilemma to share;

Death is certain for everyone but truly living your life before actually dying has to be certainly rare.

6. Captain and his love story

Serving the nation and guarding the border when we are peacefully sleeping under safe our safe roofs; There aren't enough words to offer my gratitude to those in Indian defense (The poet would like to thank every army personnel in the world for their selfless service and undying dedication).

Captain and his love story
He grew up in Kurseong, a small town yet very beautiful where he often heard the sagas of the battles and wars;
He must have been barely four years old when he picks up a toy gun and toy soldiers over toy cars.
By the time he was in his teens, he started caring less about his family and friends but read more about the Indian Defence personnel;
He had already made up his mind a long time by then and the heavens had already destined his fate's call.
By 20 he was a soldier in the mighty Indian Army and by 23 he was the designated Captain;
By 26 he had combated and accomplished several successful missions that he scarcely remembered he was also a friend, a brother, and a son.
His devotion to his country made him so focused and determined that he never lost sight of the bull's eye;
I still remember the people who had come for his funeral were mostly unfamiliar and unknown to the locals as he hadn't spent much time in his town, nevertheless, he couldn't wave his loved ones his final goodbye.

Amongst the crowd was a girl in her early 20's wearing a white kurta;
An Indian dress,

I overheard someone in the crowd whispering that girl was his fiancé who loved him so dearly and her misery can't be jotted down in phrases.

I saw the tears of his brother, and sister and witnessed the misery of his mother;

How can I ever express the tears of that old man weeping silently who was said to be his father?

The tale I just shared with you was around five years old,

I belonged to the same town where his parables are often told.

No media house covers the bravery and valor of these Bravehearts for long,

Their courageous fables are somehow lost in the wind and before one can share; It is disappeared and is gone.

But the poet within me urged me to write about his accounts of glory so a lot like him would finally or eventually get some delayed but deserving tribute;

He could have been anyone today and stayed alive but living a civilian life over the defense; He did highly refute.

7. Life beyond the 'analytical mind'

While the wanderer started his research and started seeking answers, he came across many people and visited many places. The rootless wanderer read an endless number of books and listened to many great men and women coming from every race, caste, religion, and time. Somewhere down the line, he realized the truth is in finding yourself first; Everyelse else shall follow eventually.

Life beyond the 'analytical mind'

Before we get in-depth let me assure you that the article you are reading today is fascinating yet true so make sure not to use much of your analytical mind while reading it. Be it Theosophists or those practicing Zen, the ultimate goal for them is to witness the universe at its best and become a part of it eventually which do some way falls decently close to the definition of liberation if not precisely.

Through Past life regression, Astral meditation, and Akashic records, many have claimed to find the solutions to their endless miseries and others have rejoiced to discover the key to freedom from their bondage of blockages. Blockages are often those of which we aren't aware but it does have an immense impact on our mental and physical condition which only worsens with time.

How would you feel if I tell you that there is a possibility to go back into the future, 'To that very moment, and make the things right which had once fallen apart?

Wouldn't you be excited and overwhelmed if I tell you that you may get to spend some sincere memorable moments with your beloved one who isn't with you anymore?

Well, the universe we live in is not what it looks like neither it's what we assume it to be. Throughout the ages and eras, there had been many claims made, and we have witnessed many people who had come so very close to uncovering the secrets of the mighty universe but none succeeded.

The mind is the greatest weapon ever created yet it is the most destructive one without an inch of doubt or hesitation. Imagination and illusion are not synonyms for each other as there is a thin line of difference between them and if one can understand this difference while they are practicing some higher level of meditation then for sure treasures are waiting for them indeed. Treasures of knowledge and wisdom that once received can easily change you as a person. Rediscovering yourself is what enlightenment can be termed as and the peace and bliss which comes with it can never be simply defined in words. It is purely divine and beyond expressible.

Psychological problems such as OCD, anxiety, depression, and even schizophrenia may get cured only by meditation considering one knows how to do it as doing it inappropriately may or may not have some unwanted consequences. There are said to be several realms that can be traveled by us and those worlds which are in no way like ours are mesmerizing owing to their peaceful ambiance and atmosphere. Some worlds hold our memories, those memories which we may have lived a hundred or a thousand years ago or could be even ten or fifteen years ago but have been stored and forgotten somewhere in some corner of our subconscious mind and when we can remember them, trust me, your life won't be the same again.

Saying that this topic is vast, complex, and too diversified so to understand each topic we need to read and understand it in deep and offer or allow some time to our mind to accept, process, and analyze the facts before we jump into another.

PS: The Superconscious mind is beyond science and religion and it is with and within each being but it's a myth until discovered.

9 7 9 8 8 8 7 1 7 1 4 0 1